The Lion's Tale

By Laura Buller

Editors Kathleen Teece, Abhijit Dutta
Project Art Editor Lucy Sims
Art Editor Shubham Rohatgi
US Senior Editor Shannon Beatty
Jacket Coordinator Francesca Young
Jacket Designer Dheeraj Arora
DTP Designers Dheeraj Singh, Vikram Singh
Picture Researcher Sakshi Saluja
Producer, Pre-Production Rob Dunn
Senior Producer Isabell Schart
Managing Editors Laura Gilbert, Monica Saigal
Deputy Managing Art Editor Ivy Sengupta
Managing Art Editor Diane Peyton Jones
Delhi Team Head Malavika Talukder
Creative Director Helen Senior
Publishing Director Sarah Larter

Reading Consultant Linda Gambrell
Educational Consultant Jacqueline Harris
Subject Consultant Dr. Natalia Borrego

First American Edition, 2019
Published in the United States by DK Publishing
345 Hudson Street, New York, New York 10014
Copyright © 2019 Dorling Kindersley Limited
DK, a Division of Penguin Random House LLC
19 20 21 22 23 10 9 8 7 6 5 4 3 2 1
001–311573–Feb/2019

A catalog record for this book is available from the Library of Congress.
ISBN: 978-1-4654-7913-6 (Paperback)
ISBN: 978-1-4654-7914-3 (Hardcover)

DK books are available at special discounts when purchased in bulk for sales promotions,
premiums, fund-raising, or educational use. For details, contact: DK Publishing Special Markets,
345 Hudson Street, New York, New York 10014
SpecialSales@dk.com
Printed and bound in China
The publisher would like to thank the following for their kind permission to reproduce their photographs:
(Key: a-above; b-below/bottom; c-center; f-far; l-left; r-right; t-top)

1 Dreamstime.com: Maggymeyer. **2–3 Dreamstime.com:** Capetrak (b). **4–5 Getty Images:** Jonathan & Angela
Scott. **6–7 Alamy Stock Photo:** Paulette Sinclair. **8–9 123RF.com:** Andreanita. **11 Getty Images:** Don Baird. **12
Dorling Kindersley:** Wildlife Heritage Foundation, Kent, UK (br). **13 123RF.com:** Eric Isselee / Isselee (bl).
Dreamstime.com: Isselee (br). **14–15 Getty Images:** Matthias Graben (bc). **15 123RF.com:** Virang Kundhani (cl);
Nico Smit (tl). **16–17 Getty Images:** Robert Muckley. **18–19 Alamy Stock Photo:** georgesanker.com. **20–21 Getty
Images:** Manoj Shah. **21 Alamy Stock Photo:** Avalon / Photoshot License (cl). **22 Depositphotos Inc:** Gudkovandrey
(cb). **23 123RF.com:** Petr Masek (cr). **Alamy Stock Photo:** Bildagentur Geduldig (tl); RooM the Agency (bl). **24–25
FLPA:** Ariadne Van Zandbergen. **26–27 Alamy Stock Photo:** Frans Lanting Studio. **29 Alamy Stock Photo:** Juniors
Bildarchiv GmbH. **30–31 iStockphoto.com:** 1001slide. **32 Dreamstime.com:** Brian Sedgbeer. **33 Dreamstime.com:**
Moodville. **34 123RF.com:** Simon Eeman (cl). **Rex by Shutterstock:** Jurgen & Christine Sohns / imageBROKER (br).
35 123RF.com: pytyczech (tr); Nico Smit (cl); Johan Swanepoel (br). **36–37 Getty Images:** Danita Delimont. **39
Alamy Stock Photo:** Wild Images. **40–41 Alamy Stock Photo:** Travel Africa. **42 123RF.com:** Nico Smit (cl); Anek
Suwannaphoom (bl). **43 Depositphotos Inc:** Jeffbanke (tl). **Dreamstime.com:** Jandrie Lombard (cr)

Endpapers: *Front:* **123RF.com**: *djembe ;* *Back:* **123RF.com**: *djembe*
Cover images: *Front:* **123RF.com:** Станислав Хохолков b/ (Rock); **Fotolia:** Eric Isselee b; **iStockphoto.com:**
KenCanning (Background); *Back:* **Dreamstime.com:** Eric Isselee ca

All other images © Dorling Kindersley
For further information see: www.dkimages.com

A WORLD OF IDEAS:
SEE ALL THERE IS TO KNOW

www.dk.com

Contents

Chapter 1
Welcome to the savanna

MEOW! Young lion cubs make this sound until they are old enough to roar. Most lions in Africa are born together with one or two brothers or sisters.

They might have spots and
stripes that fade with age. Cubs
stick close to their protective
mothers until they are old enough
to meet other lions.

The African savanna is home
to most lions. It is warm all year
round. There is thick grass for cubs
to jump around in. There are trees to
climb, too.

Lions share the savanna with
many other animals. There are
zebras, antelopes, buffalo, rhinos,
giraffes, and elephants. Lions eat
most of these types of animals!

Mighty male lions prowl the savanna. Unlike female lionesses, male lions have thick manes of hair around their necks. They are also bigger. They can weigh almost twice as much as females!

Male lions often paw the ground with their clawed feet. This leaves a mark that warns other lions to stay away. They use their powerful sense of smell to tell when other lions are around.

The rumble of a lion's roar can be heard from 5 miles (8 kilometers) away. The lion is the scariest animal on the savanna. No wild animal hunts it.

Lions do have to look out for other males, though. A lion's roar warns other lions not to try to harm him or his family.

Of all the big cats, lions have the loudest roar.

Lions stalk the savanna with other big cats. There are leopards, cheetahs, and wildcats, too. All cats are carnivores, which means they feast on meat.

Cheetah

Lion

A pet cat is a carnivore, too. It pounces, hunts, and rubs its smell on things to let other animals know it's there. This makes pet cats just like their wild cousins. They don't roar, though!

Leopard

Wildcat

African and Asiatic lions

Looking for a lion? There are only two continents where you can find these big cats.

African lion
This big cat stretches up to 7 feet (3 meters) long!

Habitat

African lions roam grasslands and deserts.

Asiatic lions live in the Gir Forest of India.

On the map

African lions live in a few different countries in Africa. Asiatic lions are only found in India's Gir Forest, in Asia.

■ Africa

■ Asia

□ Gir Forest, India

Asiatic lion
This lion, smaller than its African cousin, has a fold of skin down its belly. Its mane is shorter and darker.

Chapter 2
Life in a pride

Lion cubs join the rest of their mother's family when they are around two months old. A group of lions such as this is called a pride.

There are around 13 to 40 lions in a pride. The pride is made up of females and some male cubs. A small number of adult males stay with the pride. The females are all related to each other. There can be grandmothers, aunts, and plenty of cousins.

A lion pride varies in size.

Lionesses take care of the cubs and show them how to survive in the savanna. They help teach them how to hunt.

The lioness teaches her cubs through play fighting.

Male lions make sure everyone in a pride stays safe. They chase off any other lion that comes near the pride's territory.

Cubs don't get to join hunts until they are old enough. A couple of lionesses will stay behind to babysit the cubs while others go out hunting.

Male lions hunt, too. They take down bigger prey, such as buffalo. Usually, whoever takes down the prey gets to eat first!

Male lions sometimes play with cubs in between hunts.

Lion talk

Lions are the only big cats that live in groups. They communicate with each other in different ways.

Head rubbing
Lions rub against each other to say hello.

Licking

A big slurp is a way for lions to bond. Licking also helps them keep clean.

Sounds

Lions hiss, snarl, growl, and roar. A roar lets others in the pride know where they are.

Marking scent

To warn off other lions, a male rubs itself against things to mark them with its scent.

Chapter 3
Growing up

Cubs love playing. They chase each other up and around rocks and trees. They cuddle each other and roll on the ground.

Playing isn't just fun. It also helps young lions grow stronger and smarter. They learn how to catch each other, just like they will soon catch prey.

Cubs join the hunt when they are around one year old. Lions often wait for darkness before going on a hunt. They head out as a group. The lions keep themselves hidden.

They quietly stalk animals, such as gazelles. Any animal that stands away from its herd is an easy target. The lions work together to bring down prey.

Lions have special hunting skills that help them to become expert hunters. They can see in the dark to creep up on prey at night. Their strong sense of smell helps them track down nearby animals, too.

They have sharp claws hidden in their paws. These pop out to grip prey tightly. Lions also have excellent hearing to catch rustling sounds in grass where prey is hiding.

Cubs learn to hunt by chasing birds and small animals.

Prides usually relax after a hunt. Males might prowl around and spray pee (urine) to warn other lions away.

Lions and their cubs taking a nap in daylight.

Then, the lions find a nice spot for a long nap. They even nap up trees! Male lions sometimes sleep for 20 hours a day. Females can snooze for 18 hours.

A pride makes a good team, but when male cubs get older, they leave. Groups of young males, often brothers and cousins, go off in a group. The lions wander around until they find a pride to take over. They will then have cubs of their own.

A lion family

Favorite things to hunt

Lions have to hunt big animals if they want to feed the whole pride.

Gemsbok

This antelope uses its horns to defend itself from a lioness attack.

Cape buffalo

Lions pile on top of a buffalo to bring it down.

Wildebeest

About half of the prey lions eat is wildebeest, making it their favorite meal.

Giraffe

It's tricky to tackle a giraffe because it can kick back, but lions can bring one down.

Burchell's zebra

When chased by a lion, a zebra runs in a zigzag to make itself harder to catch.

Chapter 4
Lion trouble

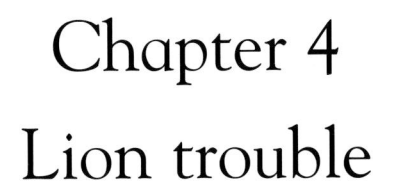

One of the main dangers that lions face in the wild is people. Humans come to Africa from all over the world to hunt lions for sport.

Farmers can also be a threat. Lions sometimes eat cattle from a farm. It's much easier to catch farm animals in a field than speedy wild animals! This makes the farmers watch out for lions and try to protect their cattle.

Other humans help to protect lions. They make laws that ban hunting. They build tall fences to keep farm animals safe. This stops farmers from harming lions that might have attacked their cattle.

The Maasai tribespeople in Kenya were once enemies of lions, but now some keep watch over them. They track the lions and make sure that they are not harmed.

The Maasai are learning to track lions using modern technology.

Lions are also kept safe in national parks. These are huge areas of land protected by governments. People can visit and learn about lions in a national park savanna, instead of a zoo.

Lions are safer in national parks than in the wild. Animal scientists can help the pride stay healthy and happy. Cubs here are sure to grow old enough to ROAR!

During safaris, people should be careful not to disturb lions.

Savanna animals

Large herds of animals live in the savanna, closely watched by lions.

Warthog
This relative of the pig has bumps of tough skin on its face to protect it during fights.

Meerkat
Gangs of meerkats live in tunnels underground.

Red-billed hornbill
This bird lives mostly on the ground, although it can fly.

Hyena
These noisy mammals live together in groups called clans.

Mandrill
This is the world's largest type of monkey.

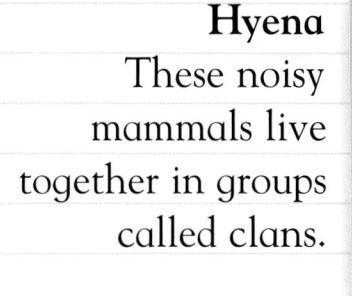

Quiz

1 What is a mane?

2 What is a lion's family group called?

3 What is the name of a female adult lion?

4 Which African tribespeople help protect lions?

5 How far away can a lion's roar be heard?

6 What are animals that mainly eat meat called?

7 How old are cubs when they join the hunt?

8 At mealtime, who usually gets to eat first?

9 Which is larger: an African or an Asiatic lion?

10 Where do Asiatic lions live?

Answers to the quiz:

1. Long hair that grows around a male lion's neck; **2.** A pride; **3.** A lioness; **4.** The Maasai; **5.** 5 miles (8 kilometers); **6.** Carnivores; **7.** From around one year old; **8.** The lions that killed the prey; **9.** An African lion; **10.** The Gir Forest, India

Glossary

grasslands
a habitat covered by grasses

herd
the name for a group of animals that live, eat, and move together

mane
long hair growing around or on the back of the neck of some animals

marking
when an animal puts a trace of its scent or urine (pee) around an area to warn off other animals

pride
a group of lions that live and hunt together as a family

safari
trip to see animals in the wild

savanna
a flat, grassy, dry habitat with very few trees

Index

A LEVEL FOR EVERY READER

This book is a part of an exciting four-level reading series to support children in developing the habit of reading widely for both pleasure and information. Each book is designed to develop a child's reading skills, fluency, grammar awareness, and comprehension in order to build confidence and enjoyment when reading.

Ready for a Level 2 (Beginning to Read) book

A child should:

- be able to read many words without needing to stop and break them down into sound parts.
- read smoothly in phrases and with expression, and at a good pace.
- self-correct when a word or sentence doesn't sound right or doesn't make sense.

A valuable and shared reading experience

For many children, reading requires much effort but adult participation can make reading both fun and easier. Here are a few tips on how to use this book with a young reader:

Check out the contents together:

• read about the book on the back cover and talk about the contents page to help heighten interest and expectation.

• discuss new or difficult words.

• chat about labels, annotations, and pictures.

Support the reader:

• give the book to the young reader to turn the pages.

• where necessary, encourage longer words to be broken into syllables, sound out each one, and then flow the syllables together; ask him/her to reread the sentence to check the meaning.

• encourage the reader to vary her/his voice as she/he reads; demonstrate how to do this if helpful.

Talk at the end of each book, or after every few pages:

• ask questions about the text and the meaning of the words used—this helps develop comprehension skills.

• read the quiz at the end of the book and encourage the reader to answer the questions, if necessary, by turning back to the relevant pages to find the answers.

Series consultant, Dr. Linda Gambrell, Distinguished Professor of Education at Clemson University, has served as President of the National Reading Conference, the College Reading Association, and the International Reading Association.